I'll Have It Here

'Hallucinatory, bursting with intoxicating images, fevered ghazals and sinuous stanzas that snake down the page – Jeet Thayil's *I'll Have It Here* is a book to savour as if it's the last book on Earth. Read it to be shocked awake in the presence of the grotesquely holy, to encounter a Rimbaud-esque *Illuminations* for our times, with end rhymes reminiscent of Blake. His lines are like scalpels; they dissect our age and cut to the bone of what it is to be human and flawed, but still insist on dreaming.' PASCALE PETIT

'*I'll Have It Here* is Jeet Thayil at his outrageous best. These are lines that rhyme flamboyantly, begging to be reborn as song, line breaks that crack like a breaking heart, arguments with the living and the dead, words to wake you up with your head sewn to the carpet. You'll have it all here: subversive ghazals crackling with dangerous laughter; elegies that go barefoot to the jagged edges of grief; poems for remembrance in "rooms you set ringing and shining at will, / mysterious rooms that are shining still".' IMTIAZ DHARKER

'What's always made Thayil a poet of global significance is his exemplary and earned recovery into joy, which is constant across this new book, partly aided by his rhythmic urgency and dexterity with language, along with an underpinning of a complex politics which leads to a highly sensual and pleasurable poetry that I've always loved and love it here. His soul is worldly and local, and his vision is a hard-earned hope.' DALJIT NAGRA

'"We disappear. We simmer." – Jeet Thayil. Is the poem the place we get to feel something we did not feel at the time? In *I'll Have It Here*, Thayil writes night poems illuminated by a "three-quarter moon" as the "close eye of the sun" revolves in its glottal orbit. Gandhi incarnates as a house gecko, and rhymes are lit as frequently as cigarettes, then ground underfoot. A possible reader might come to Thayil's book to study the vertigo of place, but also being. Here's a "stress-test ghazal", for example. But also, here's the "marvellous friend" appearing in the doorway at the last possible moment of a poem we can almost read.' BHANU KAPIL

PRAISE FOR JEET THAYIL

'Reading Thayil is like taking a fast train into the dark soul of the night. The stations whiz by in a blur. Poem on poem repeats a grim truth: everything will and must fall away, leaving in its wake a terrible beauty, the perfect artefact – the poem itself. There is a hardness to the melancholy; and, when you least expect it, a lacerating tenderness.' PALASH KRISHNA MEHROTRA

'Jeet Thayil's work is, quite simply, the genuine article. I shake, vigorously, his hand.' THOMAS LUX

'Take a walk around Jeet Thayil's brain – there's gold and grief in the shadows, guarded by beautiful, strange creatures nobody else has seen.' NICHOLSON BAKER

'[Thayil's writing] is a rich harvest; it moves with the strange and flawless certainty of a dream … and its madness is also its strength.' EDNA O'BRIEN

'[O]riginal, formally adventurous and captivating.' SALMAN RUSHDIE

'Jeet Thayil delights not just in pushing the bounds of possibility, but in smashing them to smithereens.' JOHN BURNSIDE

'One of the most engaging voices you will read, full of wisdom and regret.' THE TIMES

'[A]mbitious, wide-ranging and utterly contemporary.' TIMES LITERARY SUPPLEMENT

I'll Have It Here

POEMS

JEET THAYIL

FOURTH ESTATE · *New Delhi*

First published in India by Fourth Estate 2024
An imprint of HarperCollins *Publishers*
4th Floor, Tower A, Building No. 10, DLF Cyber City,
DLF Phase II, Gurugram, Haryana – 122002
www.harpercollins.co.in

2 4 6 8 10 9 7 5 3 1

P-ISBN: 978-93-6569-083-5
E-ISBN: 978-93-6569-950-0

Jeet Thayil asserts the moral right
to be identified as the author of this work.

The following poems have previously appeared elsewhere, sometimes in
different versions: 'Dinner with Rene Ricard', *The Paris Review*; 'Seven-Year
Season', *Red Room Poetry*; 'Wapsi', *Firstpost*; 'February 2020', 'December
2020' and 'Tears of the Rose', *The Penguin Book of Indian Poets*; 'Old', *Plume*;
'Zoology', *Portside Review*; 'You, Reader', commissioned for the French
Institute of India's Bicentenary of Baudelaire; 'Stress-Test Ghazal' and
'All Fools' Day' written live for *Stress Test* on Soho Radio; 'King Liar' and
'House', *Peril*; 'My Last Address', *Dirty*.

Typeset in 11.5/16 Aldine401 BT at
HarperCollins *Publishers* India

Printed and bound at
Replika Press Pvt. Ltd.

MIX
Paper | Supporting
responsible forestry
FSC® C016779

Adil, Arvind & Eunice

CONTENTS

I

II

III

I

DIMINISHING MARGINAL UTILITY

The first cigarette is all you've got.
From the second, it's a downhill trot.
You might as well not smoke it,
so little does it satisfy.
You might as well stroke it
like a pet, sniff it and say, Oh my!

This is the law of farm, forest and city,
rapidly diminishing marginal utility,
once learned, never forgotten,
applicable, alas, to everything,
kisses, earthquakes, the nobly rotten,
cars, guitars, bliss on the wing.

Sunsets on Mars are blue.
Sometimes purple too.
An octopus dreaming changes colour
from pale yellow to camo to black.
Its suckers light up, synapses follow.
It has a large brain and a knack

for the avoidance of pain.
I'll never eat octopus again.
Utility doesn't always diminish in value.
It can start at the bottom of the graph,
never to rise, never to accrue
gains or losses. Go ahead and laugh.

CHRYSTIE STREET

There's a Whole Foods on the corner, I hear,
a notion so outlandish, so weird,
I can't square it with that street
where food was a mistake to eat,
not whole or wholesome, just unfit.

It wasn't much of a street. An extension
of Second Avenue in its pass
across the Great Wall of Houston.
(*'House*-ton, not *hues* or *hass*,
we clear on that, hun?')

For one summer it was the famed
tenement storefront
that made an appearance in *Spiderman*,
the first instalment of Sam
Raimi's trilogy about the genius and orphan.

A scene so fleet
most viewers missed it. I mourned
Peter's exile on Chrystie Street
as I mourned my own,
and I longed for his hero's return

as I longed for my own, even if home
was gone, and my second and last wife
was almost gone, and the only thing my life
was good for was going or gone.
There was a shared bathroom

at that Chrystie storefront, a small
blue couch, a single lamp, a bookshelf
against the redbrick wall. That was all.
I read John Clare and taught myself
to smile. I did not fall

into despondency. I fell into gladness,
carelessness of youth,
a little poverty (not too much), some madness
(not too much), and a glimpse of the truth
that lay, I was sure, in the snowmelt underfoot.

I'M GRIEVING, AREN'T YOU?

So many innocent lives lost. A tragic day
for all of us, a grey, overcast, sad, sad day.
Their names we try to wish away,
and their faces – but they're here to stay.

I'm a patriot and a Republican. Let me have my say.
Not the Spanish-Civil-War-type Republican. Hey,
they weren't Republicans at all, were they?
Me, I'm American, true blue, though today

my mood's as black as my armband. I want to lay
before you some thoughts you should pay
attention to, before they're brought into play
by the politicians, whose arguments replay

endlessly in the media, who hope to fray
our constitutional rights, our national forté
– guns to defend our libertay.
For those who are no longer with us, I pray.

A mountain of thoughts and prayers in your in-tray,
people, a Mount Everest of prayers, okay?
But gun control is not the way
to fix this horrific thing. You've got to be cray-cray

to think so. We need more guns, Monday
to Sunday, at every school, church, mall and highway,
armed cops to help defray
the cost of young lives. How else to repay

your sacrifice, parents and children, but to flay
the child killer, flay him alive and shout, Yay!
I'm looking at you, abortion doc. I'd purée
your liver for sport if I could, bae.

SPEAK, AMNESIA

I can't remember why
my line breaks this way.
In November
I cracked the day
to see what might fall out.

A congealed yellow sky.
Mistake became.
In December
I saw trees in flame.
A bat with a double snout.

The president likes pain.
He's a big guy with a small, strange
mushroom for a penis and a brain.
The colours change.
Everywhere is the same.

I can't remember when
I grew these fins.
Was it now or then?
Did we sink or swim?
Hi honey, what's your name?

DINNER WITH RENE RICARD

For three years we met
at one or the other LES hovel
chosen by Tony the Dealer,
who, like all dealers,
caught kicks by making you wait
while he babied Janis,

his French bulldog,
or chose a new scorched parka
for the day,
or breakfasted at IHOP,
followed by a last leisurely snort
with his girl, Jen,

before he took the 7 into the city,
or, reluctantly, a cab,
while we waited
on the pitiful dopesick ledge
of panic.
The sicker Rene got, the meaner

his wit and cruel laughter,
but never aimed at me,
because I saw who he was,
what it meant,
the gift of knowing him.
A year into our acquaintance,

he suggested dinner
at Veselka, his favourite restaurant,
a modest meal
of Ukrainian pierogi and borscht
at nine dollars apiece.
We talked of Bonzo,

how journalists were told
not to look him in the eye
'for your own safety'.
Rene laughed, or cackled.
He said, That's me.
Don't look me in the eyes,

you guys, all of you.
I mean it, honey,
look me in the eye,
you die.
Shall we get more tea?
It's on me.

He wanted no money,
had nothing to sell,
didn't boast or brag or bitch,
except a little bit.
I knew what the dinner meant.
Now we were friends.

BLUT UND EHRE

The gods are among us.
This one says her poems slant,
laughs at her own audaciousness.
She's an accountant.
She keeps score.
At night she wakes me with a snore

loud enough to shake the heavens,
long enough to raise the dead.
Which isn't a blessing,
not just yet.
Terrifyingly beautiful. There's no denying
her beauty's annoying.

The gods among us are a multitude.
We're overrun.
Multicoloured, rude,
they're spilling out of Brixton
into the halls of freedom,
beating their incomprehensible drum.

I see them eyeing my daughter,
I hear them giggling in tongues,
not being humble like they oughta
but skipping the rungs
we were honoured to climb.
Unmask them, brothers. It's time.

LATERAL VIOLENCE AMONG
THE MODEL MINORITIES

In the interests of equal opportunity,
you propose a toast to the Pakis, 'Bom bholé,'
and remind the Injuns they're Bhangis
to the British,
whose genius was to use the correct insult
for each caste, one word
to drive us properly insane.

The city a flicker of phosphenes,
flat whispers, segregated flat screens
bifurcated by tongue or tribe or God,
and you amongst them, little vampire,
walking diatribe, starting fires,
prideful of your sodomy,
leash gripped between your teeth.

Properly insane, you stroll
turmeric-stained avenues, stale ambition,
sibling cruelties agape in the new world,
blurt of righteous chemical
three storeys tall,
chewy fog of marigold aerosol
aimed at babies in parking lots.

Nobody cares for you.
You're a cane toad,
predative, adaptive, noisy poison-eater,
satisfied or competitively middle class
when ranged among the paralysed natives,
exuberantly noxious yet lovable,
the raja, the padishah of Roosevelt Avenue.

PET SOUNDS

The Beach Boys made *Pet Sounds* in 1966.
Some critics say it's the greatest album
of all time – better than *Kind of Blue*,
better than *Around the World in a Day*
or *Body and Soul* or *There's a Riot Goin' On*
or *Electric Ladyland*. Taste is destiny.

What about albums out the same year,
Revolver or *Blonde on Blonde* or *Aftermath?*
What makes *Pet Sounds* the greatest?
A band that loved Black music made *Revolver*.
A band that wanted to be Black made *Aftermath*.
A Jewish poet made *Blonde on Blonde*.

Pet Sounds is a reminder of a gone time,
when Black or Brown or Jewish people
weren't seen. You saw us only when you drove,
windows up, through certain neighbourhoods.
You love *Pet Sounds* because this is music
before blackness entered the world.

FRIDAY NIGHT ON THE ARK

FOR VIJAY NAMBISAN

The wind pours wine, slings chansons to the palms.
See the captain, there and there, lifting his glass
to the woolly mammoths and clubfoot angels.
The seas are calm tonight. The moon's on high.
But he won't sail until the mammoths blow psalms
in reply. Meanwhile he's stress-testing the cutlass,
priming the front deck, tuning the curfew bells.
There is no right way to say goodbye.

If there were, this would be it, a night like tonight,
the moon fully lit, false calm upon the water
covering the diseased towns, people stunned
by famine and obesity, by drought and flood,
new spikes within the latest variant of fright.
Nothing ages you like the death of a daughter.
The earth ages under the close eye of the sun.
Nothing prepares you for the spurt of loved blood.

SEVEN-YEAR SEASON

WITH PASCALLE BURTON

I whisper your name and the day turns warm.
A third-quarter moon holds the father of Jupiter
in place, farther than ever, slower and meaner
through space, disappearing, simmering.

The day turns and I whisper your name,
your thousand-maned name, so terrible and rare.
In rain and in sun, I cup its flame.
Better than thinking, better than prayer.

Jupiter's father holds the moon in thrall.
You know what comes next.
One by one, the days wobble and fall.
This is the hexed season.

Slower and meaner, disappearing in space,
the world spins in circles. The worm
knows when to show her face.
'Well done,' she says. 'Good form!'

We disappear. We simmer.
The day turns from doom to doom.
In the fall, I may remember
to whisper your name from room to room.

NATURAL HISTORY

'Why do we live here?'
said the kid to a sky that rained fire.
'To ride the river, to know desire
and live in the shiver,'
he said, moving higher.

Meanwhile these words
appear as on a magic screen,
and they don't just appear, they mean
more than they seem to mean,
or maybe less, maybe they collapse inwards.

What will the wind and the tree,
the reptile on the golf link, the vivid green
parakeet, retain of us after we leave?
The earth's metallic sheen,
pink froth blowing on an inland sea?

Only the futurists kept score,
by means of handheld semaphores.
Firelight flagged our calls for more
when we measured the coastal haar.
Our HQ was windy Edinburgh.

All gone now and gone for good,
into the storm, the endless flaming wood,
helter-skelter, busy, intently mad.
The kid said, 'We been had.'
It was the end of the ... I forget.

BIRTH DIRGE

At dusk
the fields are

pitch. Unrecognizable.
We fall like

fruits from the
jamun

tree. Black
fruits burst under

their boots.
My neighbour's pregnant

daughter dropped.
The baby still

moving
gently inside her.

The men
cut

her open. The
dancers.

They dance
sitting.

Even in the
dark they

shine. One
sings while he

works. How
hard he

works. His
voice of the golden

raptors above.
Golden

voice flies
sitting.

Her
husband now.

He buries himself deep
beneath the

red soil.
His red mouth's

laugh is a small
happy

animal. The dust
rises into the

fruit of
our mouths. We say,

Our mother,
love us.

ONCE UPON A MORNING

The door opens to a hand,
open hand that waited years
to greet me, dry as the ivy
that once held this house.

Now empty but for me,
reaching for someone,
someone who's come to visit,
long after I am gone.

AS IF A LEAP YEAR WASN'T ENOUGH

Brown light at 8 a.m.
Saying, look at me, here I am,

here to remind you, son,
of those who are gone.

Summer too soon.
Soon

enough
the wind will shift

and the birds complain
re the rain,

complain loud and long,
long and loud and oh, so wrong.

Heat rings a tin
whistle round the Pygpen.

Later, a coma of cows
near the house

will quit the scene
of our sweaty Anthropocene

as I drive to the city
that hardly is a city.

I'm not alone here,
right, Galatea?

I never have been.
Don't mind me and mine,

the world is full,
that's the golden rule,

or one of them at least.
The dead are around us this East-

er.
Like you, Galatea.

Sorry, what?
I most certainly am not

hot to trot
like some respectable Hottentot.

I'm my own man,
I'll have you know. Even if I am

talking to myself at a small-town airport
bar, waiting for a spot

to open up,
to get into my cups

and let you
and your friends in teal and blue

come round and surround
me, here where the dead abound.

THE DEAD

Hidden in
ceiling

cornice or
traffic

light in a
sudden whip of

ice in a
childhood

river they
know to wait

and wait to
speak When

you're low
lowest

their voices
drip

honey into your
head

The city is
dead

and dying
It won't kill

you or make you
stronger

Better not to be
heard than misheard

Emily would
know to say

Rest dear heart
stay

this life is
sweet and

much too short

1325

Shams al-Din the Tangerine is twenty-one
when he sets off on pilgrimage.
A year or two, he imagines, then back home
to practise law like his father and his father's father.
Introducing himself as Ibn Battuta, he visits
two hundred and eleven towns and cities
in forty countries across three continents.
It isn't the pilgrimage that interests him now
but the vagaries of the travelling life.
To ride into a town and look for somewhere to stay.
To hear of a coastal city to the south and find berth on a ship,
the ship boarded by pirates,
wrecked against the rocks of a giant coast.
To be kidnapped, to escape, to fall sick
with an ailment that seems to originate in the bones.
Slowly, over days and weeks in a dim room,
over countless cups of bone broth, he is nursed back to health.
On an island in the Maldives, whose inhabitants depend
on a diet of aphrodisiacal coconuts and fish,
he takes four wives, the legal limit,
spending 'the night with the wife whose turn it was,
and this I continued to do the whole year and a half I was there'.
In all he marries ten times, keeps concubines and lets them go,
has five or a dozen children, survives a plague,
becomes a scholar, a judge, the writer
of the *Rihla,* or *A Masterpiece to Those Who Contemplate
the Wonders of Cities and the Marvels of Travelling.*

For three decades he travels. He never wants to go home.
That year the Aztecs build Tenochtitlan over marshland,
using a system of aqueducts, artificial islands and drainage.
They like to bathe two or three times a day.
In Europe, rather than bathe, they are using perfume.
Rather than plumbing, chamber pots and thunderboxes.
What they enjoy is a good war.
It's the beginning of the Little Ice Age.
What are the poets of the world doing?
Already adept at time travel,
they are futurists one day, nostalgists the next.
They are fluent in mathematics.
They know they're necessary for the progress of the race.
They don't know they'll be flattened by the meaning of money.

II

A FUTURIST HISTORY OF INDIA

Not silent like a
prayer

I'm putting on
my shoes to

step into the
streaming Time

slowed remember?
We got sick

and died
We felt the

seasons move
the sea-

sons inside the
seasons change for

worse for
good We stepped

into the reset
Now the four-

winged war
drones float and I'm

here saying
aloud this not

prayer to you
Prayer (you

say) what kind of
prayer pits

line against
stanza

sense against sentence
without full

stops or
commas whether or not

in the way of
thought? So

if you don't
mind I'll

go ahead and
laugh

– In the king's glorious new palace the poor cousin was tricked
by water so calm he thought it was land into which he fell
headlong and at the sight of the wet prince the assembled
queens' cruel laughter roared across the weeks months and
years of ruinous war that lasted eighteen days only brother
killed brother and son killed father and blood ran from
mountain to river and the winner too was lost –

Is there anything
more

dangerous than
laughter?

SELF-PORTRAIT AS FOUND STOCK MARKET HEADLINES

The market is having trouble focusing on issues that could give it direction

The market is looking for a level to consolidate on its way down

Market feels first shivers in shake-up, claws back

Stocks shrug off weak bonds and bearish futures to close higher in choppy trade

Market tumbles, reverberations expected

Market drops like a brick through impasse at its heart

Prices go into free fall, end up in the subway

Stocks close low in gloomy sluggish trade as persistent pressure stifles weak attempts at a rebound

Stocks fall off a cliff, day opens in a vacuum of sentiment

The market is very nervous. It lacks direction. In the afternoon it nosedived with a vengeance

Just how high can a dead cat bounce?

A KIND OF ANTHEM

A nation you thought you knew,
from Ashoka to Buddha to Gandhi to Nehru
in a single decade unravels into
Muslim, Christian, Hindu,
unholy trinity of saffron, green and blue,
on a field of British white.

My girlfriend's Chinese, my baby mama's a Jew,
my husband's red, white and blue.
When we're out on the toot
in Chikmagalur, Diu and Kathmandu,
there's no jealousy or rue.
We try to eat right.

We like our new brew.
We float past our differences and accrue
credit for the next Bardo. (Our karmic due!)
Either way, it's true:
We're dead if we don't and dead if we do.
Got a light?

THE GHOST OF MR GREATSOUL

Why, if it isn't Gandhi,
returned as a house gecko,
talkative, still slender,
motionless on the wainscotting.
His chirp is plummy British banter.
'Dear boy, have a dekko,

an eye for an eye makes
the whole world blind.
Or so you'll find. Mind,
one hopes not!'
(And so on and so forth.)
All I say to him is, What?

I don't mean to be rude
but you left us no food.
The carving knife you used
like some tiny god
still drips blood
on the old floorboard.

My extended hopeless family
sat down for dinner in India
and got up in Pakistan.
You turned our house into a granary
the army used for bribes
to win over the strongest tribes.

Seventy-five is three score and ten
years. Give or take five. *Years*.
You expect things to change, but what has?
Well, we pray to screens.
And they're still at it, your assassins,
in the name of love and fame.

A people divided by circumcision.
Or not. Veils or not. Meat or not.
You expect things to change the same,
Mr Gecko, Mr Forget-me-not,
Mr Greatsoul.
You're here and you're not.

WAPSI

On television the new war
blares, we sick bitches lick
our wounds and try to recuperate,
cow logic, cowed rhetoric,
cowardly assassinations replicate
the ways God dons armour

in India, in twenty-fifteen.
The earth picks at its scabs,
old wounds made fresh,
children crawl backward like crabs
to the cradle, no light, no progress,
only a cleansing of the unclean

as defined by the Prime Minister's fringe
masters. His beard drips grammar
this morning, and though his fist
pumps properly for the camera,
he has lost faith in his tryst,
his destiny, his own words make him cringe

and grieve for the gone world, the great
transformation wrought on the past,
the sly erasure of names – Nehru,
Gandhi, Ambedkar – history recast
for the age of holy terror,
the tolerant taught to hate.

Why measure time with words
when words are met with violence?
How tame, how lame this line
met with silence,
how useless its metre and rhyme,
better far to speak to the birds

whose voices grow in panic or pity,
as man's horizon narrows
with his understanding and the sun
shrinks to a tight band of porous
saffron, loud enough to stun
even him, the silent all-seeing deity.

FEBRUARY 2020

The climate's in crisis, to breathe is to ache in India.
Too cold or too hot, we freeze and bake in India.

They police our thoughts, our posts, our clothes, our food.
The news, and the government, is fake in India.

Beat the students bloody, then file a case against them.
Criminals in power know the laws to break in India.

Pick up the innocent and lynch them on a whim.
Minorities will be taught how to partake in India.

Hum dekhenge, the poet Faiz once said. But if you say it,
You're anti-national. You have no stake in India.

Women and students and poets: they are the enemy.
Come here, dear, we'll show you how to shake in India.

The economy's bust, jobs are few, the poor are poorer.
Question is: how much more can we take in India?

When you say your prayers, make sure you pick the right god.
Petitions to the wrong one you must forsake in India.

Jeet, if you don't like it here, Pakistan isn't far away.
If you want to stay, shut up, learn to make in India.

DECEMBER 2020

Twenty-twenty is acuity of vision, a bane of the plague.
It's the year we saw clearly the claim of the plague.

The poor and the powerless were first to be forgotten.
And last. How else do you play the game of the plague?

The corrupt and the cockroaches always will survive.
Home ministers too. Oh shame on thee, plague!

Mandelstam's joke about Stalin's roach moustache:
It got him sent to the gulag, a stain on the plague.

Ferreira, Gadling, Dhawale, Gonsalves, Raut –
Hounded, imprisoned, driven insane in the plague.

Kalita, Narwal, Teltumbde, Wilson, Rao, Bharadwaj,
Babu, Sen, Navlakha, say each name to the plague.

Where did conscience go in India's new gulag?
To the alley, to sell itself for fame in the plague.

Say nothing, hunker down, mask up, stay safe.
No jeet here, just your share of blame in the plague.

X-RAY SPEC

In England, sorry, Britain, we're all Asian,
which is really okay if you ask me, but probably
only if you ask me. In the American demarcation
we're South Asian, specifically and affably
monochrome, or sometimes we're Indian-American
(not American-Indian because that's a whole
other brethren) or Pakistani-American
or Kashmiri-American, though the role
allows occasional exceptions to specificity,
e.g. the Indian curry houses on Sixth Street
are actually Bangladeshi and baltis are city
pots and the old joke is still a good way to greet
visitors, that all the food on Sixth is from the same
kitchen, which is why everything is a mess of yellow,
green or brown, a transnational flag of shame.
The term *curry-muncher,* like *muff-diver,* will hollow
out gender, race and nationality, as it should.
Intersectionality is the new sisterbrotherhood.

LET'S SEE NOW, F.N. SOUZA,

Fecking Nickle Souza,
what a fecking loser,
never met a woman he didn't try to abuse-a.
But there's a lot of him in this room, isn't there?
What's that say about us? We revere
good art by bad men and women? Oh dear!

Eric Gill, Rimbaud, E.A. Poe, Anne Sexton,
et cetera, ad infinitum, anon and a-none.
Why cancel my own pleasure
and half my bookshelf for good measure
when all I'm doing in truth
is shooting myself in the foot?

Add Dom Moraes, Nissim Ezekiel, Eunice de Souza,
me and youse, uh.
As for F.N. Souza, he may be a loser and a boozer
but he's my loser.
Who are you to judge?
Pass the fudge.

POEM WRITTEN WITH DOM MORAES, TWENTY YEARS AFTER HIS DEATH

Sunday's ghost stays in bed
Scribbles poems on the wall
Trusts a future tenant
To decode his rise and fall
Does not mind the carpenter ant
Trailing dirt across the careful

Words his word-virus marries
Black coffee scarred toast
Over the day's folded miseries
You arise ghost
My own period miniseries
Offering a broken communion host

Mask mislaid by the weeping Minotaur
Your one child grown sour
Gone away pined for
Mad mother convinced she's a doctor
In the asylum she's called home these forty years or more
El Palacio del Miedo

Circles the old conversation
As the madwoman circles the yard
Waving soiled undergarments
For passers-by to parse

Berating her son the bard
La cueva de los huevos perdidos los huevos muertos perdidos

Words gleam cloth against glass
This you say Oh and this
Is the way to expire
Silver forelock in disrepair
Deifying dead friends gone wives your father
All who betray you from afar

You dropped from the ether
From cloud to weather
Made chaos forever
Visible in the wobble of Earth
No mercy or favour
But for poets detectives beer

Tenements a dirty sea construction mess
Uprooted trees around Samrat
Bandra Reclamation your last address
To Sewrie where you're interred
A distance of eleven kilometres
Farther than Father Jupiter

Jesus weeps and tells
Wears what the season sells
Propels you from reason
Refuses to listen
Says You don't get it men
It's father's fault forever amen

And the cloud on your head won't set
And the bright blue rain won't let
A woman flickers cherry wet
There by the half-open gate
Wading towards you opening wide
Long legs and splayed blue head

Pick out a coffin of new pine
Oxford buttonhole lapel pin
Imagine a slow punt friends sweet champagne
Find loud boats of vinegar wine
Twitch a tale of sin
Titled *The Burglar Saint*

Burglar Sahab envies my crutch
Lurches among God's criminals
ODs in a toilet triptych
Hoping to cast a famous spell
Wakes up infamous shunned untouched
Befriended by bottles and pills

London found you rusted you
Made you leave on a ship bound for the new
Black wind brown lookout miles of blue
Heart-shaped sail two crows your crew
Floated the mangrove coast into
Port at South Bombay

The trees your enemies
Sisters of the cleft she wears
Listen to the crash of birds
When she screams Hindi at the neighbours
Mad mother's voice in wife's mad shudder
Voice aimed at you

Then do the thing brutal and worse
That breaks a marriage unto death
Move to the suburbs
Remember to marry forget to divorce
Someone to keep you from your own best curse
Render screams to ligament to verse

Remember (she says) forgetting is key
Amnesia will set you free
The past is heat-haze hard to see
Hold a bleached skull to the sea
Fill with warm whisky
Smear out the last star smear out the sky

POSTWAR

Asteroid shower at the foot of Orion
Red crescent at my wing
Below me the earth was liquefying
I survived my monument

Recorded voices scratched the air
Mist wrapped the deck in silver
The face of the moon shadowed forever
Sky a deep blue prayer

Then came the first falling star
Waves flung themselves at the porthole
The storm was beautiful and whole
I remembered my appliances my home my car

OLD

The word went first, not the meaning
but the word, before sight, before hearing.
My hands continued to work,
just without the exaltation.
Black carved into white became an insect's crawl
across the wall, markings on a scroll
buried in a jar,
cuneiform from future Sumerians
never to be unearthed or deciphered.
Like St Gregory at the end,
how he'd take out his dentures, slam them on the table
and say, Nothing false in the mouth!
Just so, when I spoke, I couldn't hear my voice.
I was not too far gone to know
the nature of the silence that became my boon
companion. The wings of the angel of the end
near me, near mine,
lined the buoys with quicklime,
the air with tar and carbon,
then the trees fell like birds into the understanding
that we are not benefactors but gods,
gleeful and mad, who pull the world down
around us to sleep, sheet tangled at our feet.

ZOOLOGY

God's apes, we gavotte.
See Kitty under the bench,
ear turned to the trees, listening for me,
the tools of her dismemberment
in my heart if she's lucky,
in my hands when she's not.

The birds' new word is *lonely*.
The 264 regent honeyeaters left
have forgotten their own songs
and sound like some idiot new species,
says Dr Crates
of the Difficult Bird Research Group.

It's really okay, languages die,
happens all the time, what can you do?
Time is an igloo, and the sun,
the sun is high.
But the honeyeater's song is a klaxon.
He sings of us. We are his doom.

The strays whose howls mimic the street,
the orca who muscles into channels too small,
frantic for the seal's organs and eyes,
the albatross hissing, *meat, meat,*
the crows who caw and call,
and the white bear pacing his square foot of ice,

they've got the news, we kill
for joy, and die
burning down the house.

DISSOCIATIVE ID

You don't have to be blind to be broken.
Growl as much as you like, you'll leave no mark
on my mind or my art. You're a token
brown person who blights the room with dark.
Your name's a slow sickness. Your inner glider,
daft as a stain on the sun, has gone to ground,
unable to take off or find a perch or ride a
thermal to the higher reaches of the Sound.
Your guess is mine. What's the point of today?
What means meaning? Does dust follow dust?
My mother's breathing rings the hours of a day,
ragged, beatless, slow clock I should not trust.
Is there a single idea worth her half-life?
My double lives inside. Her twin too.
All night the sick flesh glows and doesn't lift.
We are long past the season of the true.
The image on the screen isn't fake or deep.
Truth is shallow. Dearest, we wake to sleep.

TINPOT REPUBLIC DAY ADDRESS

Hate will heat, will expand towards the end
of this sentence to devour your pain,
a parasite worm that eats the host's brain,
leaves a slime trail of faecal grain
and says, 'I'll be back, have no doubt,
my beautiful teeth and voice will spout
jokes, insults, news, all-caps truths about
the decline of the nation, the long drought,
the names to fight, assaults to tolerate,
violence to incite, enemies to berate,
the joys to outlaw by pleasure of the state,
constant vigil to police and infiltrate
the dubious morals of each woman and girl,
this is our duty if we're to better the world.'

DEAR NOD

Setting up my tripod
Meticulous not

slipshod
Looking

for the one nod
Letting

go the old guard
Not boasting about some

iPod
Cash kills some

short bod
Yeah

no
The son of Cush the land

of Nod
Noah's great

grandson Nimrod
I'm saying I need your

help lord
Need the staff need

the rod
Without

I'm just an odd sod
Stumbling with the

odd squad
Feeling

like a flawed fraud
Seeing

the flaming sword
Tasting

the freeze thawed
Served up like a lost

chord
Saved

from the bot bawd
Tried the book's

good word
Looked for

help from Rimbaud
Nothing works I'm slack-

jawed
First in line for

no reward
Didn't aspire to

dope lord
Uninspired on the

low road
On fire so help

me God

YOU, READER

(BAUDELAIRE)

Between boredom and disease
give me boredom or stupor or terror,
give me the disappearing trees
and fill me up, don't make me say,
More, I want more of your thin soup.
I'm not dead just yet, am I? Perhaps I am.

I've done no wrong. Wait, I'll rephrase.
I've done no wrong to you, not yet,
not when I'm playing Sad Amnesiac,
tears aimed at the last row, the cheap seats,
my eyes dry, my confessions
so shopworn you'll buy new ones.

Who's singing those mermaid ditties,
those road shanties, that lovely old smut?
Lickle Beelzebub or the Boss? I like when she tells
me to toss on past the shells, the used bodies,
when she trills, Shout if you want more,
the road's red, each step lighter than before.

She's not alone. She's a hive, a teeming lake,
a vast interlocked mass of connecting states,
alive in my brain and my smaller lung,
notched for the heart, where I draw deep down,

down into my thirst sacs her killing river
and shout, More, sister, more!

You love to read. The 86-year-old
grandmother raped by a guy pretending
to be the milkman. You like the details,
bruises on her legs, cuts on her face,
the vaginal bleeding and how she begged mercy.
All that you like, don't you, dear reader?

But you want more, more! So you pick
among the lice, grabber that you are,
giggle-monster of vice, you pick carefully,
there are too many within, though none as artful
as you, my yawner, dreamer of murder,
hypocrite reader, my lover, my twin.

III

LATE ELEGY

It's always 5 a.m. when
she returns dear wife pale
hands clasped at the window lips
askew begging to
be let in scarf still
knotted round her neck red
buds yet to flower her face

Captain Yama regent of the
back end governor
of the nether left his love
bites but denied entry What
did she expect loyalty and
respect? And what from
me left behind?

Chosen to find and
bring her down ceiling
fan awry desk meticulous but
for shoe prints room in
disarray the two of us forever
one in rage never knowing where
you end and I begin

STRESS-TEST GHAZAL

Where are you tonight, spilling your thousand tears?
Here, where you are not, each night's a thousand years.

The future's here too soon, louder than we wanted,
exaggerating each midnight's thousand arrears.

Is that you I hear, out there and coming closer,
crashing through the rooms of a thousand mirrors?

Or in the lobby of some forgotten Motel 8,
shorting the vending machines for a thousand Oreos?

Or down the lost highway, your old car humming,
white lines spun gold as you flip a thousand gears?

Or wandering the most ravenous part of town,
hunting for the ghost of one thousand fears?

Jeet, I hear you say, you'll never find me,
not even if you look among ten thousand dears.

REAL-TIME CRASH INVESTIGATION

Tonight's the night for a cheap red churn.
Three hours to All Fools' Day. Not a second to burn.
Cheap is cheap as cheap should be.
Red is red because hey that's me.
I'm drinking from the bottle. It's dark. No one can see.
One more then I floor it. Seventy miles and we're free.
You don't talk much but you are good company.

Stop signs are the enemy. I'm fine with a fine.
Cheap Sula wine is a balm to the mind.
When we hit Haryana I'll stop for a pee.
Take a deep breath and water a tree.
Swallow the taste of chemicals. Empty my spleen.
Tinkle sulphite poison on the Sea of Galilee.
I want to forgive you. But this? It's begrudgery.

I'm sorry so sorry you're dead and I'm not.
If I could I'd excise the boil on my bod-bot.
But I can't so instead consider this an apology.
For ever and ever will I be your bee.
Behind me is brunch ahead is high tea.
Remember when lunch was an opportunity?
Maybe it's time to dissolve this LLC, let me be?

ALL FOOLS' DAY

They were wrong about the dead.
If you wait, you'll see her, they said.
From the hilltop, only sapphire,
and ultramarine where three rivers met.

I couldn't wait. I spent the day lost
in water, hunting moss
agate, veiny translucent stone
that didn't show itself until I went

in solitude, blind, and met the green
world from the inside, opened my eyes
to the man I am, still alive,
all matter, never mind.

I waited for the body to float in
from the bottom or up from the side,
but it didn't, she didn't.
I waited and saw nothing.

MIND IF I SMOKE?

Dawn's late today.
Time moves like a broken mind
calmed by lithium.
What can I say
to one I lost and cannot find
through sixteen years of tedium.

Where have you gone, wife?
A promise is easy to break.
You make up your mind, drink
black milk and end your life,
give nothing, only take,
and let those who love you shrink

to dwarf shadows at noon.
Your shadow is regret.
You were gone in a blink,
gone too soon,
like smoke from a shared cigarette.
Inhale, try not to think.

KING LIAR

Even now as you lie on your stomach,
reading of the mad king, desiring me,
I know this happened a long time ago,
this room, the call of kites, the food we share
each morning, unvarying and satisfying.

I want to say, before it gets away,
last night I heard my father prescribe
the correct way to die,
without commotion, don't make a fuss.
He shuffled into my room and forgot why.

HOUSE

built of living twine
colour leeched of colour
where Ricard green
and blue enshrine

no meaning but in the things
to which her mind clings

fugue notes of living room
gusts of dolour
green paths green veins
shredded headwind

solitary bird broken
and standing like this line

FLIGHT ANNOUNCEMENT AT THIRTY-THREE THOUSAND FEET OVER NO BODY OF WATER

Ladies and
gentlemen in the

unlikely event of a
water

landing your
life-

jacket may be used for
flirtation

MODERN LOVE POEM

Your honour, the more I snore
the faster the night goes by.
The more the heavens pour
the louder the gods cry

out in their diorama.
Seeking solitude, I
prefer to bypass drama
for its opposite, a dry eye.

I'm happy to give up the house,
happy to tell you why,
most of all I'm happy now
I belong to nobody.

GENDER FLUIDS

AFTER MONICA MODY

It's a free-for-all, I welcome quitters in my cunt,
suckers, seekers, spurters, spitters in my cunt.

Write it on my skin, I want the world to know:
everyone's welcome, even mosquitoes, in my cunt.

It's a democracy, this game, the world's largest:
spinners, square-drivers, big/small hitters in my cunt.

Remember the primal, don't forget to scream.
There's always a place for Schwitters in my cunt.

I want you, and you, and you I want again.
Come in, I count all kinds of critters in my cunt.

Welcome one and all, I've prepared a special treat,
wine, violins, and mango fritters in my cunt.

One touch and I'm gone, a crazy woman
crying out loud for more jitters in my cunt.

Close the door, I'm expecting an overdue visit,
rogue income tax collectors in my cunt.

Fail once, try again, keep trying, fail better.
Join the Republic of Repeaters in my cunt.

Jeet, isn't this a form of gender appropriation?
Who died and made you queen of writers in my cunt?

TEARS OF THE ROSE

Beside me the rose
raises her middle finger.
See how she throws
love into the wringer.

Outside, the city
wakes with a start.
Don't call this art,
call it absence of pity.

The rose at the window
licks her lips,
buds of apocalypse
sail upward like snow.

Her lovely tears clog,
cascade without cease.
I'm a lucky dog.
I'm so easy to please.

MIGHT DELETE LATER

Summer left its last caress
burning on the high

laburnum blooms divining
that dirty gold tumble

to the patio tiles
where someone stumbles

drunk
I say no a lot to

visits invitations
shared sips of wine

walks in the dying
park

Wasted effort brings no
comfort in the dark

Most nights I wait Dawn
always comes

hesitant worn-
out with a

hundred complaints
All poems are love

poems
Wrong!

How is this a love poem?
How is it anything but

I'm always checking the
weather in your city

To know you can't stand the
cold and to hope

for deepest winter
where you are

TWENTY-FOUR

I loved someone
And didn't say.
Love grew wings
And flew away.

Now, each day,
Love, I say.
Too late. My dear
Doesn't hear.

WITH/WITHOUT

Conversations go nowhere.
Distractions loom, windows,
stars glimpsed from a terrace.
Stars help, but only for a moment.
Soon enough pinpricks of blood appear.
Stars hurt.

Sleep dissolves distance.
Our room at the Lutyens,
winter morning, curtain pulled,
new light on your face.
You unable to meet my eyes,
the word *love* waiting to raise

its poison head.
Without you, the minutes
run together like drops of mercury.
Quicksilver ball of peace and freedom.
Birds call, anxious for home.
Who will tell them home has moved?

FIGURE HURTLING

Darling, I was a minute behind you,
a minute behind and ahead,
time enough for a lifetime to spread
its red carpet on the pavement below,
a long way down from the eighteenth floor,
time enough for second thoughts to grow,
though I had none, not a solitary one:
a thousand lifetimes cannot compare
to this single minute we share
as I drop and the room drips on
into other rooms, other buildings,
about my head the city swirls,
speeding streets, high rise, low fall,
my used limbs loved to bursting.

MY LAST ADDRESS

Darling if you're making me a last dress
make it outrageous
so unlikely it draws sighs of pleasure
from those gentle ladies and men of leisure
my mourners
my all-day all-night sojourners
lay me out I'm saying in green satin
or velvet in A-line
and F-stop in finery on a scarred
old table that the bard
toiled upon lay me on a hill
with a view of a secret wishing-well
lay me under a tree
somewhere free as long as you lay me

SAVE YOUR BRISÉ FOR A BETTER DAY

Not like a river, it rolls like a rock,
backwards or sideways, and never unlocks.
Untamed it's a crisis and tamed it gets worse.
Time, they may call it, when we call it hers.

Singing of rivers, of talent to spare,
they called it Magog's line, you didn't dare
speak for a country abandoned, it seemed,
and never revisited but in a dream.

Budapest made you, its alphabet played you,
forty-four letters that stayed and betrayed you,
in thrall to conductors of chaos and need,
those desperate maladies scored to concede.

Ringing with light from that deep unknown well,
your face was the springboard from which we all fell,
later were hard pressed to know what was done,
what had come over us, how were we stunned?

You met every pilgrim and broke off a piece,
your mind was a tumult, your exits a tease.
All of this happened as happenings do,
without a glimmer or sense of what's true,

rushing instead like a child to her doom,
you lit up our rooms and vanished too soon,
rooms you set ringing and shining at will,
mysterious rooms that are shining still.

Out in the wildness we set up our hall,
lit by a screen, with some seating for all,
sat there unbreathing as images swarmed,
dwarfed our imaginings, goaded and charmed.

You were a story not ours to decode.
Your mouth a republic we already owed.
Your eyes told of secrets enfolded in time.
We were your acolytes, servants divine.

Your tears when you cried were like spears in my side,
receiving each word from your lips to my mind.
How could I tell them their goddess was ours,
years in the past when your fame hadn't soured?

Peace that I keep and enclose in my chest,
peace that eludes on this street and the next.
You that I speak of at song's quiet end,
here in the doorway, my marvellous friend.

ABOUT THE AUTHOR

JEET THAYIL is the author of five novels and five collections of poetry, and is the editor of *The Penguin Book of Indian Poets*.

HarperCollins *Publishers* India

At HarperCollins India, we believe in telling the best stories and finding the widest readership for our books in every format possible. We started publishing in 1992; a great deal has changed since then, but what has remained constant is the passion with which our authors write their books, the love with which readers receive them, and the sheer joy and excitement that we as publishers feel in being a part of the publishing process.

Over the years, we've had the pleasure of publishing some of the finest writing from the subcontinent and around the world, including several award-winning titles and some of the biggest bestsellers in India's publishing history. But nothing has meant more to us than the fact that millions of people have read the books we published, and that somewhere, a book of ours might have made a difference.

As we look to the future, we go back to that one word— a word which has been a driving force for us all these years.

Read.

 Harper Collins   HARPER FICTION HARPER NON-FICTION HARPER BUSINESS HarperCollins *Children'sBooks*

 HARPER DESIGN Harper Sport HARPER PERENNIAL HARPER VANTAGE हार्पर हिन्दी